BIRTHMARKS

Mick Imlah

Mick Imlah

12 Octobe 1997

Chatto & Windus LONDON

Published in 1988 by
Chatto & Windus Ltd
20 Vauxhall Bridge Road
London SW1V 2SA

Second Impression 1994

A CIP catalogue record for this book is available from the British Library.

ISBN 0 7011 3358 9

Six of these poems were first published in *The Zoologist's Bath and Other
Adventures* (Sycamore Press, 1982). Others have appeared in the *London
Review of Books*, *New Poetry 9*, *The Observer*, *Oxford Poetry*, *Poetry
Review* and *The Times Literary Supplement*, or have been broadcast on
Poetry Now. Thanks are due to Southern Arts for financial assistance
during the period in which the book was written.

Photoset by Rowland Phototypesetting Ltd
Bury St Edmunds, Suffolk
Printed and bound in Great Britain by
Mackays of Chatham PLC, Chatham, Kent

Contents

BIRTHMARKS

Tusking

In Africa once
A herd of Harrow
Elephants strayed
Far from their bunks;
Leather, they laid
Their costly trunks
And ears of felt
Down on the Veldt.

All forgot
The creep of dusk;
A moonbeam stole
Along each tusk:
Snores and sighs.
Oh, foolish boys!
The English elephant
Never lies!

*

In the night-time, lithe
Shadows with little
Glinting teeth
Whisked tusks away;
Drew through the dark
Branches of ivory,
Made a great hue
On their rapid run.

Hunters, at home
They curl up the bare
Soles of their feet
With piano-pleasure;
Sammy plays
A massacre song
With the notes wrong
On Massa's baby.

*

Out in the bush
Is silence now:
Savannah seas
Have islands now,
Smelly land-masses,
Bloody, cold,
Disfigured places
With fly-blown faces;

And each of us rests
After his fashion:
Elephant, English,
Butcher, Bushman;
Now only the herding
Boy in a singlet
Worries his goat
With a peaceful prod.

*

But if, one night
As you stroll the verandah
Observing with wonder
The place of the white
Stars in the universe,
Brilliant, and clear,
Sipping your whisky
And pissed with fear

You happen to hear
Over the tinkle
Of ice and Schubert
A sawing – a drilling –
The bellow and trump
Of a vast pain –
Pity the hulks!
Play it again!

I Have a Dream

Seen from a car on a hill near Atlanta, Georgia
Is a model of Richmond, Virginia, built out of plywood
For burning in yesterday's remake of *Gone With The*
                                    Wind;
'And that,' I lied to my friends, 'is the shell of a model
Of Toytown, Virginia, burned in the remake of *Dallas*,
A beacon of hope for the South in the *Wars of the Roses*.'

And there, in the plushest of Georgia's suburban
                                    plantations
Was the campus of All-the-John-Browns State Beautiful
                                    University
Where my own black girlfriend, after seven mint juleps,
Wriggled and jiggled so much in her seat that we gathered
We'd better pull up by some bushes that skirted the road
And would do for a loo. Time passed at a Southern pace;

And when she eventually crawled from a tangle of scrub
With a wig on (a blonde one), and tights round her ankles,
                                    weeping
That a gang of black students had jeered her and called her
                                    a 'whore',
I took it upon myself to redress the wrong
That racists and sexists too much get away with; lashed
Three twigs of magnolia into a form of birch

And found the white culprits, grouped like a circle of
                                    students
In the shade of a flowering dogwood, revising the Bible.
Civil, they rushed to oblige when I dared to step forward
The one who had called her a whore: 'Yes sir, that was
                                    me.'
'No, me.' 'You guys, it was *me*!' – Concluding together
'It doesn't appear, sir, as though any of us will admit

That we didn't immediately know she'd want to be paid.'
And slowly the doubts began to assail me there
Like bugs at the cracks in my own model relationship;
Couldn't I tell them apart, the whores and the victims,
The black and white? And what did the servant imply
With his sniggering pun on what passed for the state of
                    Virginia?

Well, as I followed these difficult turns at the foot
Of an alabaster statue of Washington Booker,
'The Black Lincoln' (or was it the other way round?),
My friends' car (a black Lincoln Convertible)
Shot suddenly up the hill and away as though with
                    tremendous impatience;
And Atlanta (or was it Atlantis?) vanished in smoke and
                    dust.

Abortion

I woke the Monday after, feeling shabby
In a ship's bed, cramped in the head with the sense
That falls in private on forgetfulness
Of parties, that of someone's shame at me;

But waiting, I began to guess, would lick me
Properly into shape. Uncurled at noon
As dry as a Dead Sea Scroll, I rose and wobbled
Blank about the cabin like a reclaimed monster

Learning to eat; and through a glassy disk
Saw even passage, sun, unpoisoning sea,
And heard the call of sea-birds hosting me
To port, and hatched an eagerness for dusk

And drink, and company. And though I dozed again,
The clock had just snored twice without alarm
When (and I thought I was dreaming) a chink
Of cups began, like washing-up:

Then with only that warning the plates
Shook on my shelves which collapsed and smashed them,
And in the immediate stillness I felt as though someone
Was sitting behind me with news of disaster.

*

Have you ever heard a noise that you think
Is unearthly (especially when you're half asleep)
But when you get it into focus it's only
Them snoring, or your neighbour revving up?

Well that's how this whirring began,
Like something familiar mistaken, becoming
As I struggled to call it a pump or the cistern
Neither, nothing else, and very loud,

Till sailors' boasts fell silent in the spray.
When we took the first buffet I dropped
My pointless jacket and almost at once
I was doubled-up in air but couldn't breathe,

And dizzy I saw an experiment
With magnets, me the broken one,
A horseshoe facing down,
Sucked up. I passed clean out

And was lucky to survive; the boat
Melted in blood, but I stiffened safely,
A rabbit's foot, gristly
In someone's cabinet.

Clio's

Am I to be blamed for the state of it now? – Surely not –
Her poor wee fractured soul that I loved for its lightness
                                    and left?
Now she rings up pathetically, not to make claims of me,
Only to be in her wild way solicitous:
'Do you know of a restaurant called *Clio's* – or something
                                    like that –
At number *forty-three* in its road or street, – and the
                                    owner
Is beautiful, rich and Italian – you see, I dreamt of it,
And I can't relax without telling you never to go there,
Divining, somehow, that for you the place is *danger* –'

(But I dine at Clio's every night, poor lamb.)

Goldilocks

This is a story about the possession of beds.
It begins at the foot of a staircase in Oxford, one midnight,
When (since my flat in the suburbs of London entailed
A fiancée whose claims I did not have the nerve to evict)

I found myself grateful for climbing alone on a spiral
To sleep I could call with assurance exclusively mine,
For there was the name on the oak that the Lodge had
                                    assigned
Till the morning to me (how everything tends to its place!)

And flushed with the pleasing (if not unexpected) success
Of the paper on 'Systems of Adult-to-Infant Regression'
With which the Young Fireball had earlier baffled his
                                    betters
At the Annual Excuse for Genetics to let down its ringlets,

I'd just sniggered slightly (pushing the unlocked door
Of the room where I thought there was nothing of mine to
                                    protect)
To observe that my theory, so impudent in its address
To the Masters of Foetal Design and their perfect disciples,

Was rubbish – and leant to unfasten the window a notch, –
When I suddenly grasped with aversion before I could see it
The fact that the bed in the corner directly behind me
Had somebody in it. A little ginger chap,

Of the sort anthropologists group in the genus of *tramp*,
Was swaddled, as though with an eye to the state of the
                                    sheets,
With half of his horrible self in the pouch of the bedspread
And half (both his raggled and poisonous trouser-legs) out;

Whose snore, like the rattle of bronchial stones in a bucket,
Resounded the length and the depth and the breadth of the
problem
Of how to establish in safety a climate conducive
To kicking him out – till at last I could suffer no longer

The sight of his bundle of curls on my pillow, the proof
That even the worst of us look in our sleep like the angels
Except for a few. I closed to within a yard
And woke him, with a curt hurrahing sound.

And he reared in horror, like somebody late for work
Or a debutante subtly apprised of a welcome outstayed,
To demand (not of me, but more of the dreary familiar
Who exercised in its different styles the world's

Habit of persecution, and prodded him now)
Phit time is it? – so you'd think that it made any difference –
So you'd think after all that the berth had a rota attached
And Ginger was wise to some cynical act of encroachment;

But when, with a plausible echo of fatherly firmness,
I answered, 'It's bedtime' – he popped out and stood in a
shiver,
And the released smell of his timid existence swirled
Like bracing coffee between our dissimilar stances.

Was there a dim recollection of tenement stairways
And jam and the Rangers possessed him, and sounded a
moment
In creaks of remorse? 'Ah'm sorry, son – Ah couldnae tell
They'd hae a wee boy sleepin here – ye know?'

(And I saw what a file of degradations queued
In his brown past, to explain how Jocky there
Could make me out to be innocent and wee:
As if to be wee was not to be dying of drink;

As if to be innocent meant that you still belonged
Where beds were made for one in particular.)
Still, the lifespan of sociable feelings is shortest of all
In the breast of the migrant Clydesider; and soon he
                                        relapsed

Into patterns of favourite self-pitying sentiments. 'Son –
Ah'm warse than – Ah cannae, ye know? Ah'm off tae ma
                                        dandy!
Ah've done a wee josie – aye, wheesh! – it's warse what
                                        Ah'm gettin –
Aye – warse!' And again the appeal to heredity – 'Son.'

(In the course of his speech, the impostor had gradually
                                        settled
Back on the bed, and extended as visual aids
His knocked-about knuckles; tattooed with indelible
                                        foresight
On one set of these was the purple imperative S A V E.)

Now I'm keen for us all to be just as much worse as we
                                        want,
In our own time and space – but not, after midnight, in my
                                        bed;
And to keep his inertia at bay, I went for the parasite,
Scuttling him off with a shout and the push of a boot

That reminded his ribs I suppose of a Maryhill barman's,
Until I had driven him out of the door and his cough
Could be heard to deteriorate under a clock in the landing.
(Och, if he'd known *I* was Scottish! Then I'd have got it.)

*

19

But of course he came back in the night, when I dreamed I
                              was coughing
And he stood by the door in the composite guise of a
                              woman –
A mother, a doting landlady, a shadowy wife –
Sleepless as always, relieved nonetheless to have found me,

Or half-relieved – given what I had become;
Saying – 'It's just from the coughing and so on I wondered
If maybe a tramp had got into your bedroom' – and then,
Disappointedly: 'Couldn't you spare a wee thought for
                              your dad?'

(I thought I was dreaming again on the train in the
                              morning
To hear at my shoulder, before I had properly settled,
'Excuse me – is this seat taken?' spastically spoken;
But it wasn't our friend that I humoured through Didcot,
                              and Reading,

No, but an anoracked spotter of diesels from Sheffield
Whose mind was apparently out in the sidings at Crewe:
Only one more in a world of unwanted connexions,
Who waved like a child when I fled for the toilet at Ealing.)

                        *

This is my gloss on the story of Goldilocks. Note:
It uncovers a naked and difficult thought about beds,
Namely, that seldom again will there ever be one
With only you in it; take that however you will.

Secrets

Where no one flushed the grass
A six-hit from the cricket,
We dealt in shallow sighs
Till hush! – she let her dress
Unbutton to the locket
And parted secrecies.

That evening, after hours,
The drink had drawn me close
To a team-mate, on a bench,
So I thought her secret ours;
And when a lull arose
I told it, for attention.

Unfit to be out naked
It lingered in the air
Like the fall of a far wicket;
But when at last he took it
With a snigger, and a glare,
And a hand across his pocket

The word was up and gone.
It spread like wildfire, blown
From ear to burning ear
Across a field of corn;
And though I sprinted home
I later sought repair

(As every charring shadow
Creeps to quench its source)
And found renewed at dawn
A cricket pitch – a meadow –
And the patch of flattened grass
A black dog squatted on.

Lee Ho Fook's

What brought the Chinaman down to the building-site?
                    Ah, it was Fate;
And Fate in the scaffolding kicked from its cradle the vat,
Thirty foot over his dithering head, of boiling and
                    thunderous tea.
Who was on hand, though, to rush from his post and
                    manhandle the fellow
(Then of a frightened, diminutive, immigrant state of
                    fragility)
Into a sheltering barrow, the moment the day's brew
                    exploded
Exactly where seconds before he'd been staring and
                    dreaming of mountains
And seagulls and sails in the harbour? Charlie Wood.

The building-site is buildings now, the Cannon Street
                    Office
Of the Hong Kong and Cantonese Bank — and all would be
                    buried beneath
Were it not for the Chinaman's blur of cross-cultural
                    gratitude:
'You have saved my life. The least I can do in return
Is to ask you to dine as my guest in my fabulous restaurant
Whenever you will.' 'Well thanks very much,' says
                    Charlie —
'I might take you up on that offer.' — Back to the grit and
                    the grind;
Thinking, though, *Tell you what, Charlie Boy, could be a
                    bit of a bonus*!

Indeed, while the mind of this builder was normally dark,
And dripping with flesh, and unwholesome, infested, and
                    spotty, a shaft
Of purest sunshine scored suddenly over the tracks as he
                    pondered his luck;
And a sluice and an avalanche opened of rice and prawns
                    like the coins in *The Golden Shot*
Churning and pouring forever and all of it aimed at his lap;
Which drew him away from the mix of cement he was
                    feeding
And up in a daze to the Works hut, and on through a dozen
                    or more
Inscrutable *Yellow Pages* – well, it would take him a
                    couple of tea-breaks . . .

Years pass. And the tiny impulse of distaste Lee had felt
At his saviour's first beaming appearance and chirpy
                    request for a knife and fork
Has swollen; of late it resembles a sort of unsociable illness
That has to be kept in check by a sidling withdrawal to the
                    stairs
Whenever his own lucky star, with its multiple coatings of
                    yesterday's earth,
Comes rollicking in for the freebies – as often as three
                    times a week.
(Something is fouling the lock in the door to his dream of
                    new premises;
Something as fixed as the bambooey bulge in Charlie
                    Wood's cheek.)

So Charlie is left to chew over the Chinaman's lapses of
honour
And nibble at rightful reprisals: *When his highness
emerges at last*
To slide me as ever the ready-paid bill on a saucer
(Disguising by this, he supposes, his part of the bargain)
What if I dashed this half-cup of their pissy tea at him —
Out of the blue, to remind him why Woodsy is here?
— Or when they've been keeping me waiting an hour for
the soup, to come out with it —
Oy, son, I had you in a barrow once — *instead of my usual?*

Crime and Punishment

It struck out, like the lash of a new clause
On a curse thought dead and buried, when he wished
His little girl of four goodnight, sleep well: –
He'd never speak with innocence again
To anyone; nor would his wishes work.

*

Kicking eventually the shallow hour's
Puddle of sleep his own face wobbled in
Disturbed this dream: the same shawled grandmother
That formerly he'd easily managed to kill
Was helpless, backed against a bathroom wall;

But every time he walloped the axe-blade
At the joint of her head and neck, the rubber head
Bounced from the impact, bounced against the wall
Like a patient rubber ball. When the rubber
Weapon sagged in failure from his wrist

The head, rebounding on its springy neck,
Addressed him freely, in familiar terms:
'But *please*, before you wake – wish me goodnight;
With kisses, please – ain't I your little girl?'
(He strains towards the lacey punchbag). BOING!

Visiting St Anthony

'*St Anthony's Bunker*, fifty miles by jeep;
Not often touristed, and very cheap;
The humble desert home of ANTHONY,
Oldest of human beings, and a saint.'

I don't remember what I half-expected
When I picked that xeroxed advert from the rest
And made my booking, to the mild surprise
Of the agent, in his shuttered, dingy room;

Long tracts of beard, perhaps, on a bony
Story-teller; or skin to prod, with a pig
Fast at one ankle; but I don't remember.
We came upon it after hours of sand.

'Mister,' the guide implored, the truck slowing,
'The saint is at his books . . .' I smelt a rat;
And sure enough, we dwindled to a stop
At what he called 'respectful' yards away

From terror, or complaint, before a sign
Whose motto's paint dribbled sarcastically:
AS THE FISH REMOVED FROM WATER SLOWLY DIES
SO DOES THE MONK WHO WANDERS FROM HIS CELL

— What 'cell'? — What pilgrim dared they hope to fool
By the bivouac of planks that Tuesday's hands
Had scrambled up to scarcely overlook
Miles of a wasted journey? Or plonked on top,

What chance that the poor beggar bound to a stool
With half a hymnal stuffed between his knees
Couldn't be dead? It wasn't cloth, but wire
That kept him blindfold, and his skull intact,

And nothing surgical that plugged the holes
Where saints have eyes. I measured up the fraud:
They'd raked this load of maggots from his thin
Pittance of rest, for my few quid – Arabs!

So much the worse my second shock. I saw
The skull, beneath its ragged hood of flesh,
Bend, like a monk's white face, as if to read;
And when, at once, it buckled and recoiled

There came a foul noise, like the waking cry
Of dogs behind the oil-drums of his door
And that was all; the pages fluttered over
Like profit counted; and the guide resumed.

'The chain leads to the Saint's devoted PIG,
Which is a thing like Mary's little lamb
Or the love of God for every hopeless man,
Whose patience is so gross, it will survive

Although the pig is very old, for a pig –
Even as old as Master Anthony.'
But there was no pig to be seen, anywhere,
Of any age, unless that hump of flies –

And I don't suppose we'd parked for a minute, before
I motioned to the guide to turn for town;
Who thought me scared, no doubt, but knew the tomb,
And was himself no chicken, as he said.

from The Counties of England

Bedfordshire

A class of ambitious young toe-rags has failed *en bloc*
To come up with a slogan that captures their county of
                                    Beds.
Each is condemned to drive off in his GT to fritter
A reasonable income on lager in Dunstable winebars.
Meanwhile, the cleaner is sifting their mound of rejections
And nodding at every half-hearted depiction of Eden . . .

Berkshire

Any day now we'll be watching the battle of Berkshire,
To be fought on boats at a picturesque turn in the water
Between (in the red trunks) thirty-six bargees from
                                    Reading
And a shimmering squadron of angels descending from
                                    Cookham.
Only the late Stanley Spencer can picture the outcome;
Only the late Stanley Spencer can ransom the angels.

Herefordshire

Another breakdown has amazed the Scoutcamp.
What can't they cope with? Bikers in the square?
Dragonflies buzzing their blue canoes, or the closeness
Of black-and-white cattle as big as Ledbury houses?
Is it the secret of beer? Or is it the arrogant
Daughters of Kilpeck, flaunting their better childhood?

Leicestershire

Leicestershire gentlemen like to be seen
Down the wrong end of a horn or a sporting gun.
The wrecked complexion blaring at the rabbit
And the notorious Grace Road bark at an Indian batting
Are products of the same inverted nightmare –
A fox on horseback riding down fat pigs.

Northamptonshire

Retrieved from the ash of a collapsed loft in Daventry
The Complete History of the County of Northamptonshire
Whose text and the numerous inserts have melted together.
For instance: 'A Family Cobbler the Choice of a Prince'
Is the heading of one of the later, industrial chapters
And 'Shoeing Britannia's March Through the Centuries' –
                                   that was an ad.

Oxfordshire

1943: working in secret, assured
That the pact preserving the beauties of Oxford and
                                  Dresden
Would be bombed flat, – Lord Cowley and others project
A magnificent *Oxford Rebuilt* on a radial pattern
With circular colleges, ring roads, and orbital
                                  cemeteries . . .
(Nuffield to Churchill: We've got the phoenix – now you
                               deliver the ashes . . .)

Rutland

Here it was always a summer evening. An obsolete
Male population of steeplejacks trail, through the
                                Uppingham streets
And the alleys of Oakham, traditional portions of
                                woodsmoke
Homewards to wives in their cottages dreaming as ever of
                                cheeses;
While over the toby-jug factory, over the orchard of
                                cherries
Creeps the abolishing shadow of wicked Squire Locust of
                                Gall.

Somerset

The musical birds who give tune to the joys of the county
Have chosen today to forsake their particular perches
Of honey and ivy at Crewkerne, and Wookey, and Mells,
And empty the comfortable echoing glades of the
                                        Quantocks
To sit with the stillness of leaves in the afternoon shadow
Of Taunton's twin towers: big Botham and Richards.

Insomnia

The girl next door won't sleep unless
A radio plays beside her head.
Ear to the door I've heard it ramble
Nights unheard; eight times the news
Repeats itself, and when at eight
She wakes herself, she turns it off.
I fiddle with a bulletin
At four o'clock, remembering Sleep
As somewhere voices cheered you up
And never said the same thing twice.

A pillow-tour; this stifling alley
Throbs with curfew lights as a lone
Reveller raps on doors demanding
Someone to talk to, someone to talk,
A hand to fix the radio. 'Streets'
He might be shouting, that or Sheets,
'Are bone dry.' Then, to no one, 'Why?'
'And where is the rain you promised? Eh?'
Along the street, a cat supplies
An answer, with a spinning bottle.

Sitting up again, I think
Of waking her, first with a bell,
To bring her padding down the velvet
Staircase unamused, the cat
Unwoken in her breast's cradle;
Or bursting in, with new fatigue,
To nudge like BOO the button OFF.
– At once, her eyes' unsheltered stare
Reveals her loss, her hearing bare
And faintness, like a blanket, gone;

But innocent, she doesn't grasp
Her bag-eyed burglar. 'Hoi, it's me,
The dread Insomniac' (I shout,
To lull her into consciousness
Or knock her out) – 'It's four o'clock.'
(No luck as yet; her hands protect
Those modest ears from boredom – still,
I know my trade.) 'It's eight o'clock.'
The yawn snaps shut! and her fooled senses
Boggle about their first dark silence.

Quasimodo says Goodnight

To think that you could go to sleep in a bed
That I made up, with hair like that unbound
On a shirt I wore last week! I should be sorry,
Esmeralda, should I? I am wicked
Sneaking back to watch you sleeping – am I?
For you cannot as you surely would express
Our difference in painful gesture; cannot
Wince, or feel for the wall, or quickly thank me
For my beans or let that pity fly
Sidelong; but now encircled by my tread
You suffer each unseen approach in silence
Or a sigh, and fumbling trespass fails because
While you pretend this deafness I can call you
Esmeralda, and you cannot think me
Beast; because I want you, and I should not.

And yet come closer; look, your mouth is open
Where a little purse of air blows in and out
And in and out; and in the mild adventure
Of a dream you cannot scale the height
To which these hands have hauled your daily fear:
Above, ten yards of tower; beyond, thin air;
Below, a wink of bonfire, memories
Of spite as faint as drowning, pale as water.
And neither does your shuttered sense admit
That you must eat my meals; that whosoever
You consider beautiful seems not
To come, though I do not mean he will not, nor
To stop him; or that I am stooping closer,
And could love you as I pleased while you
Could only hate more closely than you do.

I'd know by touching whether you were cold;
But you'll forgive me that I'm not allowed
To have a fire inside, not if the walls
Were stacked with frozen saints or riddled with devils.
The Deacon says unholy fires will break
The spell that makes the building everlasting;
This is not true he says when priests make fires
Either for light or to extinguish witches.
May I pull this blanket up? there's a gap,
You see, the cold will muscle in
And wake you up; your back is half-uncovered.

How accidental human beauty seems!
Imagine God's great metalworks, with scores
Of anxious pigmies running up and down
The length of complicated moulds with rods
And steamed-up rules and paints all day, who see
That of the flowers tinkling from the mint
Not one is blotched or crooked. Somewhere else
More hazy floats a chapel with a cage,
Where a pair of dozy journeymen play marbles
With mounds of hopeless heads: One afternoon
Exchanging nods and leers, they turn a lock
And giggling climb a circle like a stair,
And enter where they think they shouldn't, watched,
And think they steal; but from the holy pouch
Unspotted by the thief that bore it out
Is drawn and spun a careless miracle
To tease us. Beauty waits, and knows its hour,
And falls in questions: why, for one, when somebody
Great has died and I've been swinging hell
For leather on the bells, and now I've stopped
And I'm sprawled drunk on my lofty beams does the song
Of hooded boys creep up in draughts and breezes,
Chill me, and I cry, and no one knows?
Or when I saw your naked back just now,

Because in the end I had to, just at the simple
Form of it, why did I shudder and see flame?
Could you, who did it, tell me? Could the Deacon?

If we were of one element, say beauty —
Look how my fancy shuffles from the shadow,
Free of its shame, but shy to be an act,
To rouse you with a face, and not a plate,
And greet you with a smile, and get a smile;
To ease you from the crusty bedding inch
By dazzling inch, by unimagined inch;
To throw the trapdoor on new feats of air
And raise enormous fires, and laugh down loud
At crumbling roofs and chalky-haired forbidders,
And when we perished in my clasp we'd stay
And go like stone together, and be thought stone
By the Deacon, and he'd overpay the Mason,
And a new boy would toll the morning bell, —
But my beauty is all in dreams; and now you stir,
Poor angel; you have slept with me; thank you.

Cockney

How heightened the taste! – of champagne at the piano; of
little side-kisses to tickle the fancy
At the party to mark our sarcastic account of the
overblown *Mass of the Masses* by Finzi
(An aristocrat who betrayed what he stood for and set up
in Bow with his matchgirl fiancée);

Moreover, the skit I had chosen to grace the occasion ('*My
Way* – in the Setting for Tuba by Mahler')
Had even the Previns in generous stitches (it seemed an
acceptable social *milieu*
If only because it was something like six million light years
away from the planet of Millwall)

When the buffet arrived; and as we applauded the *crudités*
carved into miniature flats and sharps
There crept into mind for a desperate moment the ghost of
me mum shuffling back from the shops
With a Saturday treat – 'Look! We got sausages, beans, an'
chips!'

So I mentally told her to stuff it, and turned, with a
shivering reflex of anger
To harangue a superior brace of brunettes for their
preference of Verdi to Wagner;
But again she appeared at the door, with the salt and the
sacred vinegar

And I was reclaimed. 'You!' she demanded, 'You who last
month in the Seychelles
Took drinks with a Marquis, and studded the spine of
Lucinda with seashells –
You are the same little boy that I sent out in winter with
Cockney inscribed on your satchel!'

And as she dispersed, one or two of my neighbours were
        squinting at me as you do a bad odour,
And even my friendly advances were met by a flurry of
        coughs and a mutter of *Oh, dear* –
For try as I might I just couldn't assemble the sounds that
        came out in a delicate order:

ALL ROYT MOY SAHN! HA'S YOR FARVAH?
LEN YOU TEN NOWTS? – CALL IT A FOIVAH!
TRAVELLED IN TEE-ASCANY? – DO ME A *FIVAH*!

And worse was to follow. For over this bleak ostinato of
        base-born vowels
I detected the faraway strains of a disco remix of *The
        Dance of the Seven Veils*
And felt the lads egging me on to enact what a tug at the
        Seventh reveals –

Yes, down came the pants of old Rotherhithe's rugged
        Salomé,
And pointing it straight at the toff who was leading the
        charge to assail me
Out of my shirtfront I prodded two-thirds of a purple
        salami . . .

*

Sometimes, there's a song in my head as I sit down at tea,
        and I know what the tune is
But can't catch the words. And when I get tired of the
        humming, it's off down to Terry's, or Tony's,
A couple of pints, then across to the club till it closes, for
        snooker with Pakistanis.

Silver

Silver in block or chain
Will not sustain
    The nameless slaves
    Who row it through the waves

As long as the old, crude
Hallmark tattooed
    On every chest
    Proclaims them second-best.

Wherever the ship may steer
They face the rear;
    What lies in store
    Is untransmuted ore.

*

Breaking into the bungalow, we found
His last meal full of maggots on the cooker,
Four hundred and forty-six pounds in pound notes
In various vases and drawers,
And a bowls cup from the Fifties, silvery-brown,
By the tin of Duraglit –
He had been polishing it.

Jealousy

12 P.M.
And welcome back, at last – how dare you
Sneak out a hand like proof, extended
As though for me! Be angry? – dare you?
You dare remove that hand! Extend it!

3 A.M.
The damage dealt, these hands, unfelt,
Make fists. The faint suspicion sets,
No sooner fancied up than felt
Or dreaded, smelt. And so I settle

In a toilet, where your vicious jury
Brawl in my guts; eyes shut I call
To view the night's long injury
And pull it open to recall

You intimate behind my back.
I saw him poke a long tongue out
But only tossed a pardon back
Until I saw another tongue out,

Yours, between its active lips;
And I was in the air between,
But you wouldn't look, or close your lips
On the impudence that passed between.

I summon next your truant legs
And face, and feel but equally loth
To strike the face or stroke the legs;
For if I could muster lust or loathing,

Common fondness, anything, nothing
Fair could overrule me, nobody
Fair dismay. But you mean nothing
Until I know some nobody

Is ogling you, and through insights
Of skirt that call his eyes aloud
Is making dreams of your insides
With him in – It is not allowed!

   6 A.M.
Bad dreams. A certain smeller for proof
Nosing your door on guilty tiptoes,
Hangs, repelled by proof or disproof; –
Crawls, and fingers twenty toes;

Your sleeping bag is half-undone
And bulges with his stifled body;
As if the doing could be undone
I stoop to zip up your joint body

But out cracks his giggle like escaping
Air or a rush of mocking voices,
And I feel for my last dream of escaping
As deaf men dream of lost voices,

Or men of air in a closed bag.
I've fled now. Trailing where I've fled
My right arm drags a paper bag
Through air; now whirls it round my head;

I can't just let it hang, because
The stings would soon invade my wrist;
I can't just throw it off, because
Five fingers lash it to my wrist;

But when a pair of sticky eyes
Eye up my wrist like snailing balls
I've struck the floor — one winking eye is
Stuck to the floor, and pity bawls

At whatsisname to come unstuck
From you on the floor, and stamp on it —
But what's this salamandering grip stuck
Fast to my ankle? Stamp on it!

    9 A.M.
Good morning. What are you, a nun?
He's gone? Oh, no one — that is, no one;
You offer me your hand? No damp on it?
Take back your hand before I stamp on it!

Her Version

You judge for yourself. But I'll give you my version again:
That when I applied in advance for permission to try it
        with Mansoor
He opened the palms of his hands and I quote him *You do
        what you want,*
Then something inaudible sung as he flapped through the
        hall in his sandals;
And all that we knew of him later was noise coming up
        from the garden,
And after an hour or an hour-and-a-half the event that he
        later described
As his boomerang (!) hitting Mansoor on the side of the
        head –
He says that our features were visible there, insensibly
        staring
And mouthing out over the rockery's group of reluctant
        spectators –
In fact, at the moment the lolly-stick pipped on the
        window, for that's what it was,
We were doubled-up laughing our heads off at what was
        required of 'The Two Plaited Monkeys'
In which, if you look at the manual, the heads (does it need
        spelling out?)
Are not on the same plane; or his; well, what is his version?
That being himself a disaster in bed, everything else in a
        bed is disastrous?

Mountains

O the mind, mind has mountains . . . (Hopkins)

Snowdonian

At the start of our climbing career
Each had his flask, his blue kagul
And a uniform will to be first
In the sprint to the peak;
Nobody thought it was steep
Or fell far out of step.

So, back at the gabled hostel,
There were coffee and biscuits, a perfect
Unnecessary roll-call,
Viollet, Wavering,
White, Wood,
And no weak link exposed;

Though on the downward scree
Slipping and dying in jest
Twyford (2Y) had spotted a single
Classic sure-foot, bearded goat
Lost to the herd, broken-backed
Among heathery boulders.

Alpine

Stranded at base
When the four had gone
To grow for a gown
Frost's blue fur,

On my mind's reel
I seemed to follow
Their blurrying through
The storm's crackle

Till, wavering,
White against white,
They shivered off the screen
Like watermarks . . .

Now in the sun
Twisting blue
Daisies across
Finger and thumb,

I think I hear one
Of the frayed chain
Or the ghost of one
Baring bad gifts:

'Here are my hands'
(I think I see them)
'Violet and white
And hard as wood.'

Himalayan

Concern about our provisions was to cost us many sleepless nights (Sir John Hunt)

Roof of the world; rumble of avalanche; something
                                   attacking
The splintering walls of our matchstick lodge with
                               a vengeance;
And all I could glimpse from the sleeping bag (face to
                          the floorboards'
Powdery glass) was a snowdrift of beans, and a Nescafé
                             label, –
These were the last of our rations exploding about us!

(And it struck me again, in the hail from a cereal packet,
As when the kitchen in Ballater crackled with fire
From a fault in the toaster, the everyday nature of danger;
When even our comforts can turn, and our breakfast itself
Come in volleys against us.) And then he was there: there,
                              at the door –

There, with his featureless face at a gap in the ceiling –
Abominable, the Monster of the Slope,
Furry with frost, in the guise of a ghastly storeman:
'Get off my mountain. Get off my world.'
– Slapping huge coffee-jars into our lodge.

Polar

Sometimes all Nature seems for us, sometimes against
(Edward Whymper)

. . . For perhaps twenty minutes we stood petrified in the darkness as an innumerable dense flock of penguins swept over us, blotting out the sun and the sky, all inclined upwards as though in an aerial charge at the summit . . .

. . . The final push has been postponed again, in the wake of a horrid discovery. After good progress earlier this morning, we had slowed somewhat by noon when Hislop, who was leading, let out a series of screams, like a man who has found his skin covered with unexpected creatures. I crabbed as quickly as possible to his assistance, and though I could not understand him at first, he managed to convey by gestures that he had scraped his boot with a pick, and found *beaks*. I checked my own footing, and examined the lines of a ridge above, where the coating of blackish ice petered out like slush; and in a moment it became unpleasantly clear to me that we had been climbing in the mist on a sort of frosted mud made of penguins, for miles and miles.

. . . Morphine! and monstrous dreams . . . All nature for us or against us. I have no pictures of that bed of penguins.

?

Because it isn't there . . . I slipped and fell
A thousand feet; woke with my boots on

And the camp doctor's hand weighing my wrist
As he said gently, son, your nerve has gone.

Birthmark

On my decline, a millipede
Helped me to keep count;
For every time I slipped a foot
Farther down the mountain

She'd leave a tiny, cast-off limb
Of crimson on my cheek
As if to say —
You're hurting us both, Mick . . .

I saw in this gradual sacrifice
No end of merriment:
A broken vein or two; hardly
Memento mori.

This thousandth morning after, though
(Or thousand-and-first)
I miss her, and a bedside mirror
Bellows the worst —

A big, new, bilberry birthmark, stamped
From ear to livid ear,
Her whole body of blood's
Untimely smear.

She must have found, shaking her sock
For warnings, that the hoard was spent,
And had to stain me with her death
To show what she meant:

That it's as bad to fall astray
As to start from the wrong place.
Now I have earned the purple face.
It won't go away.

The Drinking Race

The Irish Team

Lowly, degraded things: *Guinness* with no head;
Yeats's Father at O'Donoghue's, shouting his usual joke:
'This Land of Saints' (ignored by the usual crowd)
'– Of plastered Saints'; his flies greatly undone.
Maud Gonne in need of help, lungeing between the tables,
Her great grey skirt hoiked up, abused by all;
Augusta Gregory huddling from scorpions under a
                                    Formica table,
And scaring the scorpions; *Lionel Johnson* challenging
                                    God:
'I told Him that nightly from six to eleven I perch on this
                                    barstool –
Haha!' – and over he goes; and *Yeats* in the corner,
                                    combing the heads
And the tables for bits of potato to turn into slabs of
                                    marble
In poems where his friends are made to look better than
                                    everyone else's,
Calls them 'Olympians'. (All's changed, etc.)

Brawl In Co. Kerry

I was in the bar at Castlemaine with June
Until, at half-past-ten, a word fell wrong
Between O'Leary and the little man
Who whacked glass on O'Leary's leaning head

And launched the brawl. I've memorised the barman
Lost in a boxing stance behind his bar,
And wheeling arms, and windmill sprays of stout; –
A moment's lull; then a surge, and bundling June

Flat to the bench, and the sudden pointed eyes
Under the cap across the room of the drunk
Who because we looked afraid, or young, or British
Or sober, and seemed to judge, or just because,

Threw from a sitting position his glass at us
Which struck my fending arm. Above us now
O'Leary sad from battle, howling and shaking
Blood from his shaggy head like a soaked retriever.

*

'Jesus,' Bernard groans, '– you should have thrown
Your own glass back at that bastard.' But instead
When a gap had appeared to the door we'd gone for it
And hurried stooping up the stony hill

With my split elbow. 'Look,' I teased, 'this white
Stripe is the tendon,' (meant to make her squeal);
But though she shivered like a windy day
Her face was weird with rage. She and the moon

Blinked at each other through the mottled speed
Of fugitive clouds; and from the walled-up fields
There came a sound like a host's embarrassed cough,
The formal tick tick of the tongueless cricket.

Starter's Orders

These warless days
Men without women
Thirst for the means
To waste themselves;

It's in the blood.
Their fathers worked
And Grandad breasted
A barbed tape;

But now where the girls
Are sick of courage
Men without hope
Of a job, or a bayonet,

Muster like champions
Under a canopy,
Over a barrel,
Primed for the slaughter;

Fit to pursue
Illness, dishonour,
And sponsored to boot.
Gentlemen, swallow!

Strange Meeting

As I walked down towards the Drinking Race
I overtook one combatant, whose legs
Wandered abandoned under a wet face
Rubbed ruby-red by life's abrasive dregs.

He'd jumped the gun over the rest of them
And looked a certain finalist, when he slowed
To clear his throat of the obstructive phlegm
And hailed me, as I tried to cross the road.

'You coward! You! Come here!' (He took a draught
And what he drank came straight back through his nose)
'Don't you appreciate the drinker's craft?
Why won't you stop and sup with us old pros?'

When I declined, he straightened for a spell
On his best leg, and spat from this strange stance
Like a heron proud of its own repulsive smell
Or furious at a biped's arrogance:

'With better luck, I'd catch you in a fight
Or institutional combat at the bars,
And you wouldn't know if it was day or night
For the ringing in your ears, and the seeing stars;

But meantime – that's unless you'd care to part
With twenty pence?' (I smirked) '– Meantime' (his face
Drew far too close) 'You have an evening's start,
And meet me downstairs at the Drinking Race!'

Silver Medals

Here on the last lap of the Marathon
A cruel invisible wall or wire or moat
Has baulked the Bavarian champion, and he lies
Unconscious, fifty yards from the champagne . . .

– Cut to his fiancée, winner at sixteen
Of the High Jump gold for girls at the Munich Games
(Where twelve Israeli athletes came to grief)
And also here – how did she read his fall?

But hold the replay – something's wrong; she gags;
She drapes his tracksuit over a monitor;
She sobs, at last, 'You see, –' (there at the vault
Someone's arching back) '– I know he died –'

(And for that spasm, we see a field full of him
Slaughtered in earnest: village Olympians,
Their spoons flung out to catch the spilling eggs)
'– Like in his last race, up at Helsinki.'

And again we're glad of silver medals; glad
Of easy resurrections, and returns
From the darkest hangovers; happy to share
The lie that doing your best is all that counts;

To know that the lame, the lost, the left-behind,
Even the least significant dead German,
Stumble about in the kit that Glory wears
And have their minute on the uncut tape;

That we ourselves will soon be driving home,
At dusk, along familiar chestnut roads,
To join the reel of people we've come to trust
To take no notice – only a day more failing;

That the tall West German girl was using 'died'
In the milder, athletic sense, and only meant
Her friend (*not* an Immortal of the Track)
Had finished with less pep than he'd have liked.

Hall of Fame

It seemed that from the beer-tent I escaped
Down some profound depression, where they kept

Silent the damaged and the down-and-out.
A sergeant rang the bell for them to eat,

That being the hour appointed; but the failures
Who shuffled from the darkness on all fours

Had burned away their appetite for solids
And only a couple accepted watery salads

To sip at on their disinfected bunks.
These were the veterans of such bloody banquets

Eternal headaches hurt them, and still hurt;
'Hey soldier!' I called at one I seemed to hate

Who was sitting helpless in his vest and pants
Over a tray of flat insipid pints:

'Didn't I see you when you were so pissed
On the road here, that a mug of whisky passed

Straight back out of your nostrils as you drank?
Tell me, how did a soldier get that drunk?

And how did you fare later?' Out of luck
He shed his numbered shorts and made me look

At something that I wished I had not seen,
The ruined arse-hole, flapping, crudely sewn,

Through which he spoke: 'After the rout – I lost,
I think, or won – came either first or last –

'They bore me up, oblivious to my wound,
On eager shoulders; but before they could be warned,

'With a loud noise, the crap larruped down my leg.
Now every Christmas I raise half a lager

55

'To absent friends; and absent is the word,
For nobody loves me in the Drinking Ward

'Or brings me chocolates or forget-me-nots . . .'
So moaning he withdrew; the last three notes

Blew like reveille from their fading source.

The Zoologist's Bath

'Among the more eccentric exponents of evolutionary theory
... [was] ... Arthur William Woolmer (1833–80). His most
controversial thesis, detailed in the posthumous *Decline of the
Mammal*, that land species, having descended from sea-going
forms, would strive to return to their original element, won few
adherents ... His "crowning race" would have been the mer-
man.'
(T. A. Paish, *The Sciences in the Victorian Age*, 1949, p.139.)

I

It happened as I settled after Partridge came
With the tea and my petit-point, which she'd cleverly
                                                found,
So that I was arranged with all the things I would need
For an ordinary week-day evening's entertainment;
And Arthur had gone up to take his bath.
How did I know? The noise was not excessive,
And years should have got me used to the once queer
Begrudging scrape of the staircase door, and yet –
Like a clock that ticks its way through a steady childhood,
And then, as the family sit by the fire in all
The assurance of what they are known to enjoy, stops,
And frightens them more than the dark or a wild man –
The door and the business of whispers now, when the
                                                house
Should prefer to be quiet, had me out of my rug in a second.
Partridge was biting her pinny, and the new man bossy,
Insisting 'I shouldn't go up, miss' – my own brother,
He seemed to be saying, would want to avoid needing me.
I was up the flickering stairs in a moment and running
Beyond the awakening tentacles and startling teeth
Of the landing gallery and into his bubbling chamber
Where such was my rush and conviction of aid that I
Saw him before I could hope to avert my sight.

57

2

The same thing happens every time I bathe;
Something about the tumble of the water
On my blunted toes, or the sense of home I get
Watching the slow waving of my little hairs
Like reeds above a monster, sets me off.
I know it's not the popular idea
Of scientific method – getting wet –
But neither's raking up what the wind brought down
For Mrs Newton; neither's making tea
Somewhere in Scotland. Think of Syracuse,
Whose greatest minds, as Gelon's *Chronicle*
Of Ancient Sicily records, would rise
Each dawn, and gather in a school, and home
Like clever lemmings on their natal club,
The civic lavatory. ('Laboratories'
Evolved in ageing Caesar's deaf left ear
When ships brought him; and since his sad mistake
We've toiled in smelly rooms for little drops
Of stuff that's on tap everywhere – the truth).
But Syracuse! I see their happy wise,
Each in his lukewarm tank and smirking down
At something raving in the square below –
Hot-blooded Archimedes doing physics –
Now they duck under with a nod, and will bask
Knowingly till sunset. When I feel
My bottom buoyed, and start to think of fish,
I am at one with them; and furthermore
As Catherine says it keeps me pretty clean.

Well, what I see at first is a tap or tube
Like that big loopy rectum the koala hides,
And out of it streaming a stuff like creamy pupae,
Thick with little eyes, and full of fins,
Splashing into the water and diffusing.
This generates a wonderful parade
Of landed species bearing liquid children,
Or frankly, shitting fish. I'll see a pheasant
Issue unshelled spawn, a cow discharge
Its mackerel in pats, a vivid worm
Crack as the pike slides out. And suddenly
Hypotheses will rocket round my skull
Like starfish rolled by gulls across the sky;
Are not the night secretions of the tern,
For instance, like an oily saw-dust, sign
Of the discreet development of gills?

Surely the Hebrew Sages knew about it –
What happened to the fish in Noah's Flood?
Had they no sin to choke for, that the world
Became what might be called their oyster? Did two
Of each variety (and Holder counts
Five hundred thousand submarine divisions)
Angle themselves? Did Noah's little boy
Devise, one drizzly breakfast while his dad
Was lecturing the lions and the dodos,
A warm aquarium to sleep a million?
He didn't. Germans have mapped the Bible's truth
Meandering out of Science into Symbol;
How could you justify a family
Of *eight* to countless legions of mere pairs?
We must assume that only two were human,
Including, I imagine, *Shem*. Discount
The nagging *Wife*, a medieval shrew;
And *Ham*, the pig that none of them could eat;
Sore in the seed of the drowsy baby hummed

The order *Iaphetoptera* (wood-wasps);
And the paragon, Old Noah, was a whale.
Try proving it? You're in the Deluge, right,
And someone says, I'll bet you drown, you're wicked;
What would you splash to, an ancient ape with a
                                          hammer
Or a hulk with a mouth the size of Crystal Palace?
Of course you would. Remember when we read
The Other Testament that its skull-capped bards
Had motives of their own, religious ones;
No journalist wrote Genesis; no Jew
Would think of other species. Noah's ark
Was Noah, the chosen mammal. Evidence?
The eye-witness account appears in *Jonah*,
Those ghosted memoirs of the bashful Shem.
(Nor can we swallow in the modern age
The biblical account of what took place
At the Red Sea; it occurs to me that Moses
Was vestigially amphibious; his tribe,
Adaptable; the Egyptians, stony lizards.)

But these are only signs; and did our God
When feastless we moaned through Sinai, when our nets
Strayed loose on Galilee, torment our sense
With whispers of manna, bulging basketfuls
Of shadow? Nor shall our appetite for fact
Go belly-aching; we have tongued the flesh,
Abused it, called it man, and hooked it up
For the sharp winds and the centuries to hurt,
Till eating it at last we give it names
Like 'bread' if we are Sunday Methodists
Or 'fish' if Friday Catholics, who stand
Like bullies on the hilltop, nearer God.
Nor in the days of His ministry was Christ
Ever unsilver, ever coarse with hair

Or long in the open air. Two points should seal it;
First, did He walk on water? Did He need to?
And secondly, what emblem did they choose,
His persecuted followers, and why?
And does not man aspire to that? Do I?
I wrinkle, underwater, in ten minutes.
Before the hour, I shall have a fin.